Pray My Favorite Saints

REV. LAWRENCE G. LOVASIK, S.V.D.
Divine Word Missionary

PART 2

CONTENTS

Nihil Obstat: Sr. M. Kathleen Flanagan, S.C., Ph.D., Censor Librorum
Imprimatur: ✠ Frank J. Rodimer, J.C.D., Bishop of Paterson

The Nihil Obstat and Imprimatur are official declarations that a book or pamphlet is free of doctrinal or moral error. No implication is contained therein that those who have granted the Nihil Obstat and Imprimatur agree with the contents, opinions or statements expressed.

SAINT ELIZABETH ANN SETON
First American-born Saint

1774 – 1821   Feast: January 4

✦ ✦ ✦

SAINT Elizabeth Ann Seton,
you were a woman
of strength and courage.

You were devoted to the poor
and educated the young.

Help me to value my education
and to realize its importance
in my life.

Encourage my love of those
less fortunate than I am.

✦ ✦ ✦

Did you know?

Saint Elizabeth Ann Seton was widowed and left
with five children.

In 1808, she established her first Catholic school in
Baltimore.

She founded the Sisters of Charity.

SAINT JOHN BOSCO
Patron of Editors

1815 – 1888   Feast: January 31

✦ ✦ ✦

SAINT John Bosco,
you were from humble beginnings
and lost your father
when you were very young.

You knew hardship,
and you chose to grow from it.

I ask you to be with me and guide me
when I feel lost and afraid.

Give me strength and purpose
when I am unsure where to turn.

✦ ✦ ✦

Did you know?

The mother of Saint John Bosco consecrated him to
the Blessed Mother when he was born.

He is known as the Apostle of Youth.

He is the founder of the Salesians.

SAINT DOMINIC SAVIO
Patron of Children

1842 – 1857   Feast: March 9

✦ ✦ ✦

SAINT Dominic Savio,
you lived a simple life
of study, prayer, and duty.

In spite of poverty and ill health,
you were kind, cheerful,
and helpful to others.

Please help me to live my life
with a song in my heart.

Show me the way to reach out
to those in need
and to give them comfort.

✦ ✦ ✦

Did you know?

When Saint Dominic Savio was five years old, he
learned how to serve Mass.

He studied under Saint John Bosco in Turin, Italy.

Pope Pius XII made him a Saint in 1954.

SAINT MARK
Patron of Notaries

Died 1st century A.D.   Feast: April 25

SAINT Mark,
how fortunate you were
to write about the life of Jesus
and to know Saints Peter and Paul!

I pray that I learn to spread
the Good News of Jesus
by my words and actions.

Encourage me to practice my Faith
in Jesus.

Did you know?

The Gospel of Saint Mark is likely the first of the four Gospels to have been written in Greek.

He was the cousin of Saint Barnabas.

He is represented in art as a lion.

PAX
TIBI
MAR
CE

EVAN
GELI
STA
MEVS

SAINT CATHERINE OF SIENA
Patroness of Nurses
1347 – 1380   Feast: April 29

✦ ✦ ✦

SAINT Catherine of Siena,
you looked beyond
the things of this world
to the divine life.

Help me to remember
how important it is
to pray every day.

Guide my steps to do
what is right,
even if others
hinder my efforts.

✦ ✦ ✦

Did you know?

Saint Catherine of Siena was the youngest of
twenty-five children.

Popes Gregory XI and Urban VI welcomed
her advice.

Pope Paul VI declared her a Doctor of the Church
in 1970.

SAINT ANTHONY OF PADUA
Patron of the Poor
1195 – 1231   Feast: June 13

✦ ✦ ✦

SAINT Anthony of Padua,
you were tireless
as you preached boldly
and served the poor.

I ask you to help me
to learn from your example
and to look to the poor with love.

Thank you for showing me
how to be good and kind to others.

✦ ✦ ✦

Did you know?

Saint Anthony of Padua was actually born in Lisbon, Portugal, and given the name Ferdinand.

He became a Franciscan in 1221.

Pope Gregory IX declared him a Saint only a year after his death.

SAINT THOMAS
Patron of Architects
Died 1st century A.D.   Feast: July 3

SAINT Thomas,
you may be the reason for the
expression "doubting Thomas,"
but you also were a man of courage.

Help me to remove my own doubts
and to be a person of Faith.

Give me the spirit
to pray as you did:
"My Lord and my God!"

Did you know?

Saint Thomas was one of the Twelve Apostles called
by Jesus.

He was called Didymus, which means the "twin."

He was martyred in India.

SAINT BONAVENTURE
Patron of Franciscans
1221 – 1274   Feast: July 15

✦ ✦ ✦

SAINT Bonaventure,
you were a man of peace and unity,
devotion and enthusiasm,
prayer and action.

Please watch over me
and help my daily attempts
to learn lessons well,
show charity to others,
and be humble in all I do.

✦ ✦ ✦

Did you know?

Saint Bonaventure was a good friend of Saint Thomas Aquinas.

He wrote the life of Saint Francis of Assisi.

He was made a Saint in 1482 and a Doctor of the Church in 1588.

SAINT CLARE
Patroness of Television
1193 – 1253   Feast: August 11

✦ ✦ ✦

SAINT Clare,
your life was one of prayer,
silence, and fasting.

Show me how to embrace
the spirit of poverty
and an unselfish manner with others.

Encourage in me a habit of self-sacrifice.

✦ ✦ ✦

Did you know?

Saint Clare was the spiritual daughter of Saint
Francis of Assisi.

She was foundress of the Order of Poor Clares.

She endured illness for many years.

SAINT MAXIMILIAN KOLBE
Patron of Prisoners
1894 – 1941   Feast: August 14

✦ ✦ ✦

SAINT Maximilian Kolbe,
you lived during
a tragic time in history.

When I am met with unkindness,
I ask that you give me
the deep love
that you had in your heart.

I pray that I might have the courage
to put the welfare of others
before my own.

✦ ✦ ✦

Did you know?

Saint Maximilian Kolbe became a Franciscan priest
in 1918.

He died in a concentration camp at Auschwitz in
Poland.

Pope John Paul II declared him a Saint in 1982.

SAINT MICHAEL
Patron of Policemen

From dawn of creation   Feast: September 29

✦ ✦ ✦

SAINT Michael,
you are a beautiful spirit
   of light and love that surrounds God's
      heavenly throne.

Please watch over me,
   keep me safe,
   and protect me from evil.

Be with me
   as I praise the Father
   Who is all good.

✦ ✦ ✦

Did you know?

Saint Michael is an archangel.

He successfully led the forces of heaven over the
powers of hell.

He is honored as protector of the Catholic Church.

SAINT ISAAC JOGUES
North American Martyr

1607 – 1646   Feast: October 19

✦ ✦ ✦

SAINT Isaac Jogues,
you desired only to bring Jesus
to people who did not know Him,
but they treated you cruelly.

I hope that I may turn the other cheek
when others are mean to me.

Better yet, help me to reach out to others,
even though they treat me unkindly.

✦ ✦ ✦

Did you know?

Saint Isaac Jogues was born in France.

He became a Jesuit missionary.

He and his companions died at the hands of
an Iroquois tribe.

SAINT CECILIA
Patroness of Musicians

Died 2nd century A.D.   Feast: November 22

✦ ✦ ✦

SAINT Cecilia,
I admire you
for keeping your word.

I ask you to help me
to be faithful to God,
especially when it is most difficult.

Please give me the strength
always to stand up for all my beliefs.

✦ ✦ ✦

Did you know?

Saint Cecilia was born in Rome.

She converted her husband, Valerian, to
the Faith.

She was martyred because she refused to sacrifice to
false gods.

SAINT FRANCIS XAVIER
Patron of Foreign Missions
1506 – 1552   Feast: December 3

✦ ✦ ✦

SAINT Francis Xavier,
   you willingly traveled anywhere
to spread the message of Jesus.

Wherever you went,
   you preached, taught,
      and helped the suffering.

I may not travel far,
   but I ask you to help me do my part
   by praying for missionaries—
   for their safety and their success.

Did you know?

Saint Francis Xavier was born of noble parents in Spain.

He joined with Saint Ignatius Loyola and others to form the Society of Jesus, also called the Jesuits.

His missionary work took him to such faraway places as India and Japan.

SAINT LUCY
Patroness of the Blind

Died 304 A.D.   Feast: December 13

✦ ✦ ✦

SAINT Lucy,
you are a model of faith and purity.

Please help me to see
how important it is
to lead a good life.

Help me not to sin
when I find that would be
the easy way to act.

Thank you for your example.

✦ ✦ ✦

Did you know?

It is believed that Saint Lucy was born in Sicily.

Her name means "light."

She met her death by the sword.

Prayer

THANK You, God,
for all the Saints.

How wonderful to have
so many people to look to
who can teach me,
inspire me,
encourage me,
guide me,
pray for me,
love me.

I pray that I will learn from them
how to live a good and Faith-filled life.